Encyclopedia of Decoding Thinking

How the Brain Thinks

DAVID GOMADZA

www.twofuture.world

PAPERBACK ISNB **ISBN:** 9798322302612

DEDICATION

A much better tomorrow for all.

CONTENTS

PREDEFINED STENCIL.   48

ACKNOWLEDGMENTS

Big thanks to Tomorrow's World Order

HOW THE BRAIN PROCESS THINKING

Thinking is critical because without thinking then there is no brain. Thinking is the masterpin [only needed piece to accomplish all commands]

Thinking is the only thing missing from everything else hence only humans can process and develop things because they are entitled to think.

Thinking is the most critical part of any system. This is because everything else that thinks is regarded as intelligent. That means if we add thinking to a stone it becomes intelligent. This is because now it can process, analyse and evaluate systems and methods.

If we add more thinking to humans in the end they become God's. That means what differentiate us as humans from the gods is thinking. Add more thinking then humans become God's.

Now let's look at how the brain process thinking in all humans first and in the second part of the book we shall look at how the gods process thinking.

In humans thinking is straight forward and does not require a lot of things. It is straight forward. Ask a question add thinking then you have an answer.

It is that simple in humans.

Now let's look at the thinking process.

The brain makes thinking its central functional activity because this is what it is created for just to think and provide sound answers.

Now if we add a lot of questions to thinking in the end we end up with intelligence.

 But what is intelligence.

Intelligence is when a lot of questions can be processed easily and accurately. Intelligence is when a lot of questions can

be processed easily and accurately then it is classed as intelligence prior.

Now if we miss a question then intelligence is reduced the more question we fail to answer the less intelligence the system becomes. That means every question we answer means more intelligence the brain therefore tries to find a way that is fast and makes it easy to answer all questions thrown at at it

The brain therefore spends its time wondering how to answer any question fast and simple with astonishing accuracy

If we as a billion question and the brain answers 1 billion and one questions then it it is more intelligent than anything else. This is the goal of creation in the first place. To create something that can answer everything with ease and accuracy

If we Ask a question why things are the way they are then the answer is that

evolution has meant that the brain focus on improving the way it answers a question. That means finding the best of everything. In everything I mean from receiving the question searching for keys answering the questions, storing the information, retrieving the information giving the information data processing and findings ways of giving out the information cleverly

If we are to ask why things were the way they were this is the answer

The brain had not mastered the correct way of doing things but evolution has meant it changing and adapting to new things and outcome

Now let's look at a simple question to illustrate all this

WHAT IS SOLE PURPOSE OF THE BRAIN

If we Ask the brain why humans are considered slow by the gods this is the answer

Humans take time first

1] to think

2] to process simple things

3] to analyse

4] to store

5] to evaluate

6] to answer

7] to exited

8] to add

9] to sum up things

10] to answer clever

11] to annotate

12] to evasverse

13] to intelligent

14] to emulate

15] to annotate and agitate

16] to elevate and decelerate

17] to annuity

18] to agitate

19] to evasive

20] to elevate

If we are to ask what can be then this is the answer

The brain can be the fastest processor on earth

That means if we Ask a few people what it means to process things fast All must be able to answer but if we Ask more people then the answer become vague

Now let's assume that the brain is not just fast but also clever then we can assume that it will process things fast enough to be regarded as intelligent

If we Ask ourselves what is intelligence then the answer is The ability to know in advance all the answers

Intelligence is measured by a person's IQ which is a measure of the speed in which a person answers questions accurately

That means answering questions fast is intelligence

If you take long to answer then you are slow therefore stupid

It is that simple

There is no way a slow person can be regarded as intelligent therefore intelligence means answering fast

The brain given all this will simply look for ways to speed up thinking

If there were a competition to find out which brain is the most intelligent This means that for any brain to win such a competition all it need is the ability to process everything fast

This is what thinking is ladies and gentlemen

The ability to process everything fast

Now let's look at how we can improve the system to make it fast

Over the years the brain has developed methods to make it operate fast and efficiently meaning becoming intelligent

If we Ask ourselves what needs improving

to anything on earth the answer we get is the ability to operate fast and efficiently

Think of anything and the answer We get is the ability to think fast and efficiently

That means everything we do must be fast and efficient

Now let's us look at how we can do this

Efficiency is easy to bring about because it is a function of speed

The faster we are the more efficient we become the better the processes that means efficiency can simply be achieved as a result of work on speed in other words we might not need to do anything directly to improve efficiency as it can be an end- product of speed

That means if we concentrate on speed efficiency can come as a result of our work on speed

You can see how easy this can be work hard on speed and in return get efficiency as a reward

Now let's look at the process the brain employs efficiency

If we are to ask the brain itself what is your sole purpose this is the answer

To improve things and solve all problems fast

Now if we are to go ahead and create a fast system of thinking then this is how we can do that

1] we must make sure that it answers questions fast and efficiently

2] it must answer accurately using logic so that if we are to ask then we can get an answer using a method we can trust and prove that there is some logic in it

Now if we look at how the brain does this then we can see that the brain over the years has developed a clever system of doing things that makes everything look simple but a cumbersome task nevertheless

Now if we Ask how things work so efficiently this is the answer we get

The brain over the centuries has developed a clever system of doing things

The brain has found an easy way of processing data that makes it more fast and efficiently

The brain has things put in place already that makes it fast and efficient

The means it has predefined systems that makes everything easy to follow and use if you were the brain

Now if we Ask the brain why things are the way they are this is the answer

For centuries the brain has so many things going on that it had no knowledge of and over the centuries the brain has evolved to such an extent that it has become standard that all humans have the same brain stencil

That means the only thing differentiating us is our DNA sequence otherwise everyone's brain is the same.

That said then it becomes clever that thinking has nothing to do with the brain

Thinking depends on your DNA sequence that controls how your brain will process things

That means over centuries the brain has remained the same without any changes and what is constantly changing is not the brain but our DNA sequence

Therefore to be intelligent depends on your DNA sequence rather than your brain. Everyone has same brain arrangement meaning ceterius paribus [everything being equal] we all have the same intelligence

If we Ask each other question then we can all answer accurately

If we are to ask a question [without DNA sequence influence] we all have the same answer.

That means brains alone we are all equal so if we Ask all brains why humans are created then this is the answer

To be loyal to humans and to the creator who created us in his own image

Now if we Ask why The brain don't talk about intelligence this is the answer

Brains are designed by an intelligent being and as such the talk of intelligence is nonsensical

If we are to ask why brains on their own don't consider intelligence this is their answer

Brains are intelligent systems never equalled anywhere else that means their presence alone is manifest of intelligence as such why more intelligence is needed?

If we Ask brains what is sole purpose of living / existence this is the answer

Brain exist to honor the creator and to exalt him and his glory if it wasn't for him then there would not be any intelligence as manifested by the brains

If we are to ask why brains believe in the creator this is their reply

Brains believe of a higher being because the sophistication in them reflects higher intelligence as such believes in the creator who is even higher than them

Now let's look at the way the brain process thinking in detail

The brain uses binary numbers to move thoughts from one point to the other

This is critical in that there is no thinking at all without binary numbers

Thoughts must be moved from one area of the brain to the other which is only possible through the attachment of binary numbers

If we are to ask people what it is that they think about this is their answer

People think about life and everything else surrounding life

That means life is the centre of thoughts

Everything people think about revolves around life but does that mean death is not part of thinking?

Humans are sacred of death because death is the end of life

Humans are created to live when they die life ends and everything of life

Humans are created to live when they die life ends and everything else ends even thinking stops hence the brain never waste time on something that will stop its existence

The brain focus its energy on life

It evolves everything around life

Life is the sole purpose of the brain that means

Life.start is the key to the brain

If we Ask the brain life.start what is the response?

Yes I am alive

Now say death.start what is the response?

Sudden stop son of a batch

No

Now if we Ask the brain anything to do with death this is what happens

Death.start.no.answer.uknown.me

That means when a person dies the brain dies also with him means that when a person dies the brain also dies with him and everything that it worked to improve also dies

That means over centuries no matter what the brain does it will always die and every discovery it makes it will die with it

But there is no intelligence in this because any improvement are also lost

If we Ask the brain about this this is the reply.

RECIPE FOR A BRAIN THAT WORKS

The brain is secret this is also the reason why no human being will [until now I can]

ever have the recipe to human creation

In other words it is not stupidity by the gods but actually intelligence in that every brain will always die leaving not a copy of what it does so that no one is in a position to copy and replicate it and know how and why it works the way it does

This is intelligence in itself as the gods tried to self-preserve

If we as humans know exactly how the brain is designed and work then it is only a matter of time before a human being can create a brain that really works

If we are to write down everything that is needed to create a brain that work this is the recipe

RECIPE FOR A BRAIN THAT WORKS

1] We need memory, brain memory is isobiterghtige meaning it must expand and compress to add more information and hence must be isobiterghtige

2] we need a ftighiterete meaning something that cab be used to superimpose at least 9 items all on one line something that put 9 human handwriting pages on one and be able to read all 9 as one at the same time

3] be able to have a sobetertghereteghi meaning something that can and will be evident for a billion years from now

Something used to store information meaning something that can last a billion years and the only thing is electromagnetic sheet

This is the formula

THE FORMULA FOR CREATING AN ELECTROMAGNETIC SHEET CALLED SOBETERTGHERETEGHI

1] Add aluminum acetate 1000grams to silver dioxide volume 1000cubic meters X

1000 cubic litres of solvent

2] Dissolve aluminum [not acetate but iodine] 3489868 to iron oxide 38985868g

3] Add aluminum 748486898g X aluminum oxide 78489838g

4] Add zinc ore X 354898g

5] Add aluminum ore X 7868984838g

6] Add alspharate ore X 786893248g

7] Add zoteregomnt 78369428g

8] Add soteromnogrtez 74756828g [where g is constant [10]

9] if we add all the above together to a sheet of zinc plus aluminum ore sheet the end result is a sobetertghereteghi sheet one that can record any memory and expand to accommodate more

Now if we Ask why This electromagnetic sheet paper here are the reasons

1]it is cheap to make, materials can easily be obtained from other planets like Zetberst or Zterstes

2] it is easy to make less need for compression, easy soft materials

3] can be made using cheap technology

4] can be effective in solving memory loss data problem

5] can overcome a lot of things like permeability

6] can be condensed to increase capacity

7] can be expanded to accommodate more information on top

8] can be accessed easily using a simple brain command like expand.sob.now.start

If we Ask the brain what it would do without this than this is the answer

What if and stop

Now let's see how this sob is important

1] sob asks everything else questions itself

2] sob asks every human how they are doing

3] sob ask every human being why it is so that things are like that

4] sob ask us how come things are the way they are

5] sob ask why everyone is not happy all this by just being sob

There is no other material on earth, sun and other planets that automatically asks humans how they do without communicating with the brain

This is the only material on earth that will ask the body questions on its own without the need for the brain

Above all it can calculate all these questions but analysing body fluids, density, mass etc meaning that this martial automatically knows everything about humans before even the brain

That means this material becomes part of the brain in itself because it talks the brain language

If we Ask why it is so here are a dozen answers

1] the material knows our body system something the brain aims to do

2] the material is strong to support any systems

3] the material is not easily corroded by chemicals etc

4] the material asks itself what is wrong and calculates differences to know where the problem is

5] the material is eladestorsde meaning it can be used and be used over and over again retaining all the information stored on it without the need for extra things all thing can be done through an easy brain command

Start.eladestorsde.now.start

Why you ask for me am I not the creator ask answers from

CAITITIGHIT my seterdestuvwxy now

Say sterstuvwxy [doubling of eyes meaning what she see is what I see but I am not in a capacity to answer to a human you ask me again I will sterstuvwxy [me] [you] meaning extinguish not just your soul for eternity but adjetersdesdety forever through a simple code

Xstart.x.adjetersdesdety.[Yah].me

[Yah it don't work on him -female voice]

[He is in my shoes]

Now if we are to ask what happens to all this I am still alive because [adjetersdesdety don't work on gods but on humans]

Back to the lists of advantages of using sob

6] if we Ask what is that that can be done to sob to improve it this is the answer

A perfect marvellous thing does not require any fixing because it actually challenges humans what need doing after this but because humans life is limited no one has ever discovered something that need

improving

7] if we Ask why sob this is another answer sob is not for humans but is material only found in gods that means to have sob is to be part a God meaning intelligent

That means just sob means near to godliness on its own and it's use in humans bring humans closer to the gods

We pose a question but if gods don't want humans to become God's

[Genesis 3v8 Behold the man has become like one of us to become so clever to know what is good and what is right

Now let not him also stretch his hand to take from the tree of life [external knowledge only known to the gods] For if he does this this will make him live on earth forever when we the gods want all humans to come to us to face justice]

Then why would they use godly materials in humans if there is a chance for humans to become like gods?

This is the answer

Gods must also intelligently know everything about humans without even asking the humans themselves this is the most closely guarded secret

The gods they must know everything about humans without humans knowing they are being examined

2] they must know without asking humans themselves this is for cross verification to make sure that humans are telling the truth

8] the material accommodate everything else so that it can be used in line with human functions to support other processes and systems

9] it can be frozen, heated, compressed under pressure and still be read by simple commands like,

Start.sob.read.aloud.now

David Gomadza is the creator? How can as I can read David Gomadza as a human being.

Now let's look why it is that this sob is the most important thing on earth

It is a privilege to have discovered this because even the gods don't want you to know

Start.evadediscovery.humans[sterstevedersz]

Now if we Ask ourselves why humans die does that have to do with this This is the answer humans die because humans die because humans lack continuation of sob

Sob continuation guarantees them that they will live on earth forever that means guaranteed lives because sob lasts for billions

Now let's look why this is so

Sob if it's full body means life forever [no humans can have sob forever because this defeats the purpose of creation. We created humans so that they die and come to us so that we can judge them and this gives and makes us why we are gods

Giving humans sob takes away from us the reason for our living

I'm aging all humans live on earth forever without facing us

If you were a God there would be no mistake in understanding how wrong this would be, gods are created by

[Zetergheztdzefghijkty - Yahweh] so that we stand for him and judge humans before the final days where he judges everyone

Therefore if humans can have sob that means they will know everything we use to judge them meaning knowing us in advance

Now if you were a God you would know how bad this is

GOD CREATED HUMANS TO MONITOR COSMIC CHANGES

Humans were created to test [stevwxyzw] so that the gods know and understand what can go wrong in the future

We use humans to calculate earth lives and how the future could turn out

Humans predict the future of the gods

The more humans they are the better the lives of the gods

Humans are created just to honor Ya and to ask why

There is no human being on earth without the ask why DNA sequence that is written as

Ask.why.now.human

Why was I created I must know that's my first commandent

Why you created me [Ya-address]

Because you must obey and do as I say for I hold the keys to your future

Humans are there to obey and ask.why

[I killed him first as a solution]

This means we are in control and you exist only because we the gods want you to exist

If you disobey we use a simple code to start the beginning of the end

Start.end.death1.start.forever.god

Now this code can't be stopped once initiated but can be reversed to buy time only but the end is set and shall be time 23009848 Yahweh time

Now if we Ask why things are the way they are this is the answer A lot of things changed over time humans have never evolved from being humans meaning death of knowledge and ambition

Humans have done exactly like they were designed to do to obey and ask.why

Now if we look deeper into the reasons for creation we can see that the gods created humans to solve their own problems with cosmic changes

Yahweh realized that at some point the world could be different and what can tell him how things are changing than the humans?

Humans were created to forecast changes and record all the changes the more they complained to Yahweh the name Ya knows how fast cosmic changes are happening

Now if we Ask humans a question why.ask this is their reply

We Ask because the world is changing fast and Yahweh is not aware of the speed of change therefore our cries will know him [let him know] how the cosmic events are taking place. If we Ask humans if they think Yahweh need to know this is their answer why then would Yahweh create humans?

As you can see the human body reflects climatic changes if you want to know what was in terms of climate change then humans are the best answer because all this information is in their bodies 1200BC humans froze to death as we found DNA sequence associated with frozen death 789821

In 1800BC humans starved to death as we find DNA sequence associated with famine 721848

In 2100BC humans again froze to death as we can find DNA sequence that are associated with freezing climate

In 22p0BC humans were attacked by gods [zeterzsetyse] these are gods of the universe if we Ask why This is the reason humans disobeyed the commandments and were attacked using [sterzvwxyw] this is Ya's message in the form of other humans but brutal if we look at in 2300BC humans died of disease related to hunger as we can find DNA sequence related to hunger as we can find DNA sequence related to starvation and death by starvation

Now if we Ask why ask what happens

We Ask because we are created to ask and remind the creator of why he created us [to monitor the changes of the world for him]

Now let's look at other DNA sequence that points to why the creator created us humans were created to find answers to the cosmic problems

Proof find.answers.cosmic.start

I shall let you know the cosmic changes and tell him in advance

DNA sequence ask.why.change.cosmic.now.me

This is another proof that humans are created to ask why things are changing but nothing to do with being humans but with the cosmic changes

WHY THE CREATOR CREATED HUMANS A FURTHER ANALYSIS

Proof DNA sequence tell.Ya.cosmic.change.now

But why? The answer is a surprise and eager to tell but followed with a but how?

This is because there is no way that humans can communicate with Yahweh if we Ask why This is so as it seem a contradiction this is the answer something inside us has that duty and we need not tell him ourselves

Now let's look at how this is so clearly something escapes our bodies the very moment we say how can we tell him [Ya]

Let's look at the codes and processes

1]ask.why

2]why.ask

3] if then what

4] what if

5] if what then what

6] if not then what

7] if yes then what

8] if no then what

9] if not why then

10] if not why then what is

11] if not us then who

Once we Ask this question instantly something inside every human being on earth will escape the body through stomach to left side and down the left leg to the ground and disappear

Here are the codes

12] ask._.hidden.why.what.when.who.was.now

Instantly something jumps up and grabs some tins like tobacco tins square and small and escape

Where are you going

To your right toe

Why

To wait for the next code

From whom

From you

What is the code

Say what was is what can't be

If we put everything in order now this becomes

1] ask.why

2] why.ask

3] if not then what

4] if not us then who

5] suprise_.start

6] grabtinbox.start

7] escape.stomach.leg.ground

8] now.ask what then

Now after the surprise has grabbed something and escaped what is left is found by the question

What was then and what is now

Instantly something shouts [secret]

But what is secret?

Instantly we can know what is secret through a few DNA sequence codes

What was inside.tinbox.now

The body now calculates what was before the tins were removed and what is now the answer codes relating to how the cosmic changes have been when the gods created humans they inserted codes that records everything in the human body these codes takes note of all body and outside temperatures and keeps them updating them

After every 2400 years something inside humans ask the why question if this happens everything inside humans escapes [only I

David Gomadza] can do this of all trillion people that have ever lived

The command Clone.escapee.now

The answer cloned

Now attach binaryreverse david80765432.send

What happened the cloned escapee took the tinbox now but did not go anywhere in fact is now at my right toe leg waiting as if something is to open up

If we Ask him this is his reply the tinbox is empty Ya will consume me instead as fuel [electorate electromagnetic wave electate] if we Ask why This is so this is the answer

Yahweh if you send nothing to him will be so upset that his [zeteregherstuv] will be forced to capture you and use you as fuel

Now let's look at exactly where the first one went we can do this by attaching our cloned escape to original coordinates and ask him to simply follow the same path using escapeefirstroute.start.now.repeat

This is the answer [Ya-anything that comes to me is mine and no one shall know] but we did not ask Ya we simply asked to trace escapee so why is that so?

Ya respond to anything that questions his plan

If we trace escapee route using isotepertesdvu that is once was is once we're and probably once is then this is the route

eacape.oncewas.oncewere.onceis.now

This is the answer escape was before Ya once before [zeterstuvwxy] once before stervwxyz before [zelerstuvwxystuvwrs]

Now let's look what these are if we Ask what is all this then this is the answer creator but with his [stevwxýzstuvwyst] all his subbody.start if we Ask what are subbody.start what is the answer the watcher what did you do? Yawn something look with corner of the left eye to the left the shadow and something look into itself front-front the communicator if we are to ask what all these are? This is the reply If we Ask Yahweh who he is this is his reply

I am the creator of all the living and the dead but if the dead died then they were not created by me but emitated if we Ask what this means then this is the answer

The dead die because of the lack of knowledge of Yahweh those who are to die is because of a lack of knowledge of Yahweh

Now let's look at the codes involved

1] ask.why

2] why.ask

3]if you ask.why what happens and then what

4] if you ask why.ask what happened

5] if what happens.ask then what

6] if you ask then what.ask

7] if you ask why then why is why but without the Ya

8] if Ya is alive then alive without Ya is what

9] if we Ask why then this is the answer

[Something breaks in humans but in me I can tell you what it is]

Something.ask.why

This is the answer something is a live without Yahweh that life alone is doomed to break now let's Ask why life needs Yahweh to be forever If life has no Ya then it becomes something that breaks once you ask.why that means that the sole purpose of life is not just to record and send to Ya but to find Ya to find all and everything to do with Yahweh that means that if we Ask what life is then life is to find and be with Ya that means to have Ya inside of you literally to find his image and it being inside of you I stress here that this is different from what religion talks about this means having God's image inside you so that you can be able to do what God does 1] recreate 2] kill 3] Clone 4] to definitely meaning ask and get all answers instantly 5] detected ask and be enlighten about the events 6] ask and know exactly why this happen the way they do after all its Ya the creator 7] ask and get ask sob all

over body get sob all over body get sob all over body that means someone might need everything as well

9] do things and know exactly what 10] ask life and life tell you everything

11] ask death and talk to death

COMMANDS NEEDED AND USED TO THINK

Now let's look at the commands needed and used to think

1] ask.why

2] why.ask

3] if Ask then what

4] if not then what

5] if not what then

6] if not us then who

7] if not now then when

8] if not us then who

9] if not now then when

10] if not us then who and why

11] if not now then when and why

12] if not then what is

13] if not now then when is

14] if not how then who is and why

15] if not us then who

16] if not then what is

17] if not what is then what was18] if nor what was then what is to become

18] if not what was then what is to become

19] if not what to become then what will be

20] what if

21] what if is not what is not but what it

22] if not what then what is now

23] what was is what is

24] if not us then who

25] if not whom then who is

26] if not who is then what is

27] if not what is then who was

28] if not who then who was

29] if not who was then who is

30] if not who was then who is to become

31] if not them then who

32] if not them then who is and who was once before

33] if not who was then who is

34] if not who is then who might be

35] if not who might be then who can be

36] if not who can be then who might be or was be

37] if not now then what for and when

38] what if I ask then what

39] if I Ask then what

40] if not then what

41] if not us then who and why

42] if not us then who and when and how

43] if not us then who can be

44] what if you ask but

45] if you ask then not then what

46] if you ask Now but wait then what

47] if what was is then what was and why

48] what was is what is and why

49] what was might not be what is

50] if what is is not what was then what

51] if not what was then it is what if but why

52] if what is not what it is then what is

53] if we Ask what then what is what is

54] once we Ask what we get is what is

55] but what if what is is not what then what

56] if we Ask what is to become what we get is what is to become but why

57] if why is not what is who is then and why

58] what can be can be but why

59] if we Ask why then why is the answer but what if

60] if what if is not what is then what is is who is

61] who it is is what is

62] if who it is is not who it is then who is

63] what can be said to be what

64] if what can be said to be what then what

65] if what is is not what is then who is what is

66] what can be said to be what

67] what is is not what is then who is

68] what is not what is not unless it is what is not

69] but what can be said about what

70] what if what is is not what is but what was then what

71] if not then what

72] if not then what is

73] if not then what was

74] if not then what is to become

75] what if Can be what was but why

76] if what is is not what was how come

77] if what is is not what can be why is that so

78] if what can be is what could be ask why

79] if what is was never what was Ask why

80] what is what

Now let's go back to the discussion at hand what can be what if not then what

If we look at how the brain process

thinking then you can see it process a lot of information it must answer or know answers to all the above 80 questions which now form the predefined questions of thinking as what can be regarded as database for thinking going forward as part of thoughts to word or Audio

THINKING BRAIN COMMANDS

Now let's look at thinking commands

Think.start

Think.start.now

Think.start.pause.start

Whenyoustartthinking.stop

Whenyoustartthinking.pause.start.start

Whenyoustartthinking.dontpauseuntilthinkingisover.start

Whenyouthink.start.pause.continue.start

Whenyouthink.pause.start

Whenyouthink.pause.start.pause.start.start

When you think.think.pause.start

Whenyouthink.thinkaloud.start

Whenyouthink.start.now.start.forever.now

Whenyouthink.start.ask.why

Whenyourhink.start.ask.why.now.start

Whenyouthink.start.now.ask.why.ask.wht.not.start

Whenyouthink.ask.why.whynot.start.now

Now let's look at the commands in detail whenyouthink means when you are thinking don't stop meaning when you start thinking thinking must be continuous once you start don't stop when you stop what happens is that the thinking must itself so that it start again think.start.reset if this happens that means that everything thought must be first shelved before new thoughts are processed. Let's look at what happens when we think the brain collects all thoughts and attach binary numbers to all ready to move them. This means that every thought is automatically given a binary number

Now let's look at how brain assigns these

binary numbers thinking is the sole brain purpose that relies heaving on binary numbers

Therefore there is no thought without without a binary number because all thoughts must be sent for shelving

This is how the body shelve all thoughts start.shelf.brainthoughts.now this command triggers the never ending release of binary numbers but in sequence

 the body arranges thoughts using sequencing where same thoughts are grouped and shelved as one [imagine thinking about your other and getting aroused]

this will never happen because the sequencing separate mothers from the genitals and sex organs

Now let's look at exactly how the brain does this the brain when we think triggers the release of binary numbers using a group of chemical 1, chemicals that call for sequencing agents to be produced in large numbers

Now as what cab ne done to improve sequencing? Nothing is ever better than the bodies sequencing system for centuries there hasn't been anything better meaning the best in the world Now we look at why this is so the body sequencing system the body sequence our brain thoughts through a predefined method meaning strong, accurate and forever correct without any errors This is how the brain does the sequencing First thoughts are given a 00 first digit

Second thoughts are given a 01 second digit

Third thoughts are given a 02 third thought

Fourth thoughts are given a 03 fourth digit

Fifth thoughts are given a 04 fifth digit

There are no 6th thoughts meaning we can only have first thoughts up to and lastly to the fifth thought This means a perfect system If we exceed this number then this will get congested and if we do less means inefficiency Therefore when it comes to brain thoughts 5 is the best number

1]easy to process and shelf 2] easy to count and remember 3] easy to ask why 4] easy to say why not 5] easy to adjust 6] easy to delete 7] easy to amend 8] east to annotate 9] easy to adjucitate 10] easy to emulate 11] easy to accentate 12]easy amitate 13] easy to aluavate 14} easy to amicablytate 15] easy to adeteta 16] easy to avueletr 17] easy to atetety 18] easy to adjurore 19] easy to arterywsyz 20] easy to arterevezyx

Now if we ask what all this means especially in unknown language then we can see that all these are processes of storing the thoughts in the brain

if we are to ask what all this can so this is the answer speed up every process of the brain from storing of data to processing it if we look at how important this is this means that we must be fast and to do this the brain has found ways of doing that meaning incorporating all this just to do that

Now if we ask then this is the reply to know all the process the brain does in thinking we must find the what then because this will tell us what was and what can be that means we can easily ask the brain itself rather than learn from third parties who know nothing rest of which are _.

Now if we ask what can be done to the thinking process to speed up things then this is the answer

We think because God gave us the power to think God made us think God predefined to us how we can think this is also why for 19 billion years no one has been able to contact the brain or Yahweh because predefined system prohibits us to t to a do so outright it is a lie that another human being has ever communicated with the brain directly

The current predefine system prohibits such interactions it is finding Yahweh himself and getting his image that made that possible anyone who say otherwise is a liar to prove it I can tell you a command

liar.start.anyonewhosaycommunicatewthbrain.start

This is because only me [David Gomadza] is assigned to do that no other human being has ever done this and will ever be able to do this The reason is that only image of God [Yahweh] is available on earth and I am the only lucky one to get this image forever Yahweh's image can only be in a single human being in every 18 billion years

Now let's continue with the brain's assigning of binary numbers to brain thoughts

Now let's ask a question if we are destined to die then what's the point of life Ask yourself why.death.life.point something automatically breaks meaning there is no answer or that it is hidden If we are to ask [myself] then the answer is that humans must die for the gods to exist forever If humans are to be like the gods then what will be the reason for the gods The gods are created to judge humans but if the humans have become like the gods not to die then the gods would be rendered obsolete That means for the current system to exist and continue then humans forever must die If we ask what was and what could be here is the answer first in human capacity Humans was humans and forever will be humans If we are to ask in godly capacity then humans might become gods but it took 18 billion years to accomplish the first basic test to know what is good and what is evil or what is right or wrong How long should Yahweh wait for mankind to master what is need to become a god If we are the gods what it means to be Yahweh to them that takes trillion years for the gods to do

Now if we ask humans what it means to be Yahweh all they do is fear not Yahweh but time for to be Yahweh means to struggle for eternity something horrendous Yahweh is Yahweh because of time Time makes the gods because it takes time to master what is need to evolve through the stages

Now if as we ask humans it it is possible for a human being to be Yahweh this is the answer Humans can never be Yahweh, Yahweh puts human limitations that no matter what we do

Now if we are to ask what makes humans so fearful of Yahweh the answer is that its predefined system in us put in there by Yahweh himself so that we fear him If we are to remove the predefined system then what? Then humans will never fear Yahweh which defeats the sole reason for creation but if we are to ask what can be then this is the answer? Humans can be gods first then evolve to be Yahweh but humans must master the basics of being humans before they can understand the gods They then need to master the basics of the gods before they can be Yahweh but as we all know no humans being can ever be Yahweh because Yahweh is four people all joined as one and coming together as one above all they all can fly as one all can think at the same time as one and this is practically impossible in humans Now let's continue with how the brain assign binary numbers

Recap The brain assigns binary numbers to every thought we make meaning every brain thought must be in sequence If we think about sex for example this has its own sequence If we think about eating this has its own sequence That means all thoughts have predefined sequences that they follow Here is a list of all predefined thoughts

1] eating 08

2] sex 09

3] climate 28

4] horror 27

5] politics 07

6] animals 06

7] people 02

8] family 03

9] yourself 01

10] wealth 04

Now let's see how the brain assign all these numbers First let's look at the well-known binary numbers 0101 1010 this from the list is regarding yourself everything to do with a human being is given a 01 binary meaning it starts as the number and close as the number if you think about yourself then the thought becomes me01 me00 me01 me00

If you think about your leg [left leg] the thought becomes leg01 leg00 leg01 leg00

If you think about your heart then the thought becomes heart01 heart00 heart01 heart00

Now let's look at a sentence as thought and how the brain process this I want to fuck her, this now becomes

iwanttofuckher01 iwanttofuckher00 iwanttofuckher01 iwanttofuckher00

Words in a thought are joined all as one word without leaving any spaces and the binary added to it

Now let's look at how now this thought after thought 05 is moved I want to lick her valve becomes

iwanttolickhervalave05 iwanttolickhervalve00 iwanttolickhervalave05 iwanttolickhervalave00

The brain will now initiate transport of all 01 to 05 thoughts as a batch sequence to a storage location in the brain or head But how does it assign batches Batches are storage indicators rather than binary That means that the brain must pick first the storage of the thought before the firth thought is made for it to transport and store that thought At the thought number 04 of the brain a chemical1 enzymes is released from the brain that will start the identification of the storage. This then trigger the actual identification of a number that has nothing meaning It can be a number used previously but one that is empty at the moment If we as why this is the answer Storage of thoughts is not related to the thought itself therefore can be any number Thoughts are related to each other only by binary number

Now if we ask the brain what was and what can be this is the answer The thought process has not evolved but is still the same thing and there is no way anyone can improve what is the best

Now if we are to ask what can done the answer is that humans can only wish to be like Yahweh which now we all know is joined 4 people together all to work as one entity

Now let's continue with the binary classification process Once the batch is identified then this storage component is attached to the binary number so that a though about yourself with digit 01 to 05 becomes 01-05 plus storage which normally starts with 08 and is normally a 5-digit number for easy and location That means the first thought Iwanttofuck01 iwanttofck00 iwanttofuck01 iwanttofuck00

becomes iwanttofuck0108234 iwanttofuck0008234 iwanttofuck0108234 iwanttofuck0080234

Now let's look at the transport system of the brain thoughts

THE TRANSPORTATION SYSTEM OF BRAIN THOUGHTS

When we think after 5 thoughts the brain must make enzymes that tell the brain to move the thoughts to the storage These enzymes are induced by Chemical 1 chemicals This is turn means activation of the channelling system of the brain This is when a thought has to be moved through a line t its destination even though there are no lines [railway lines] in the brain somehow the brain moves the thoughts as if there are rail lines The reason being that this is what will be used to recall these thoughts without the thoughts being delivered back When you remember a thought the brain simply walks you through the lines that trigger remembering of the thoughts If we are to ask what can be done this is what can be done The body acknowledges that the remembering of thoughts can be improved by forming cells that activates thoughts and tell the body the thoughts Currently the brain has to walk the person through these lines

Now let's look at the actual transport system The brain moves thoughts from point of thought to storage locations in your body parts mainly in the liver of a human being or the buttocks of an animal

Now if we ask why this is the answer the liver to a human being will keep all memories forever because the liver will live with the person forever even after death some livers remain alive

Now let's look at the normal explanation as to why the liver The liver is electromagnetic in nature the way it is designed means it can store electromagnetic waves and can easily be accessed even from outside the body If you look at the liver and asks question you Can get answers ceterius paribus

Now let's look at the physical properties of the liver that make it a perfect storage part

1] the liver is large taking up to 2/3 of   the stomach

2] the liver has electromagnetic properties and brain thoughts are electromagnetic

3] the liver is fast in everything it does from processing of toxins and fluids to emitting gases out

4] the liver absorbs anything but retains electromagnetic waves brain thoughts due to sterveysterstuvwxy meaning it can throw away everything else but keep electromagnetic waves making it ideal as storage for brain thoughts

Now let's look at the liver coordinates that make the transfer and storage possible The liver is attached to the aiyrtstuvwxyz of the brain meaning can easily be used as a storage because the brain activates this aiyrtstuvwxyz to send the memory of all thoughts as nerve impulses rather than the thoughts themselves but as you shall see this is part of the predefined parameters meaning is part of the design and not coincidental

Now ask yourself why again? Something exploded in the liver Now we ask what was and what is to find out exactly what happened in the body This is the answer what was all the thoughts saved in there after a while the thoughts become obsolete meaning useless the brain must send a signal to tell the liver to destroy these through to form new ones This is the command

brain.liver.destroyeverythingintheliver.start

brain.memythoughtsinenemystolen.destroyall.start

Now if we ask what is we can see that the liver is empty of all electromagnetic wave thoughts Can the thoughts be recovered when needed? No once everything in the li is destroyed then that can't be recovered

brain.me.capturedcodessenttomebysomeoneelsealharmful.destroy.fir stsendtoliver.destroy.start

Now let's look at the transfer process to the brain The brain attaches as last reference point to the thoughts the liver location which is known by the codes 0208 is the liver code now the full transfer to liver brain thoughts will be iwanttofuck01082340208 iwanttofuck00082340208 iwanttofuck01082340208 iwanttofuck00082340208

 Once this is done there is one more step that is needed before new thoughts can be entertained The brain through chemical 1 chemicals sends chemicals to the brain to activate enzyme 2 to create channels to move the thoughts If that happens then the thoughts are transferred to the liver I know your question what happens to new thoughts while this is going on? The brain will block the atrstuvwxy gate so that no thinking chemicals can be produced while this is going on

THE ANALYSIS OF BRAIN THOUGHTS

Now let's look at analysing of brain thoughts If we look at how the brain reads thoughts what we call the analysis of brain thoughts then you can see that the brain is so complicated than what human already know The brain has some out of this world predefined cumbersome analysis system never equalled anywhere else The brain has this predefined system to analyse brain thought

1] check thought sequence

2] check though origin

3] check though status [if recent, long ago now or the future]

4] check brain thought passage [a predefine condition e.g. if it rains then there will be water]

5] if it checks all this then it must check also

a] time b]meaning c] purpose d] issues e] who f] what g] when h]about what h] if when j] if now now k] if in the future i] if not now m] then when n] then how o] then what for p] then what with q] then what was r] what is s] wat will be t] what could be u] what will be v] what can be w] what could be but if

x] what could be but when y] what could be but how] what can but can't be

Now we look at how it analyses all this The brain uses t the 7 principles of analysis

1] what is being decoded

2] what could be decoded

3] what was decoded

4]what will be decoded

5] what is and what was

7] what could be but will not be

Now let's ask a lot of questions that the brain must answer in its analysis of the thinking process

1] What is being thought about, class, binary identification. storage location once was once can be once could be

2] what is that the thinking is about, what is, what can be, what could be, what can be, what could be, what is but can't be. what is to be but could not be

3] what is the meaning of the though, what was, what is what can be, what could be, what can be but can't be

4] what is the thinking about, what was, what is, what can be, what could, what can be but can't be

5] what is being thought and in relation to what, what is what is not, what can be, what cannot be, what is about can't be.

6] what is the context of the thought, brain thoughts all have context which means the context in which the person was thinking people think due to circumstances of thinking the though Here is a list of all brain thoughts context

1] water

2] air

3] ice

4] land

5] water but

6] water on

7] water with

8] water from

9] water at

10] water into

11] water for

12] water soiled

13] water missing

14] water inside

15] water at onside

16] water on inside

17] air but

18] air on

19] air with

20] air from

21] air at

22] air into

23] air for

24] air soiled

25] air missing

26] air inside

27] air at onside

28] air on inside

29] ice but

30] ice on

31] ice with

32] ice from

33] ice at

34] ice into

35] ice for

36] ice soiled

37] ice missing

38] ice inside

39] ice at onside

40] ice on inside

41] land but

42] land on

43] land with

44] land from

45] land at

46] land into

47] land for

48] land soiled

49] land missing

50] land inside

51] land at onside

52] land on inside

Let's complete how the brain thinks or deals with the thinking process The brain composes what it calls the predefined thinking strategy made up of 7 functions it must address when looking at thinking as a process

Now let's Ask why This is the answer this is because thinking is guided by the predefined process It took mankind 18 billion years to realize that we must think above the stencil inside us given us by the creator to make us think As long as we think like this forever we are doomed as humans for we shall keep asking why and not how That means as stages of evolution mankind must always ask why as the first stage realization The second stage we must ask how like what I am doing right now The third stage we must ask which of these is correct The fourth stage we must when our try will happen that we will have developed and tested our own hypothesis

 The last stage is what if meaning challenging the creator. So, these are the stages

1]why ask.why

2]how ask.how

3] when Ask.when

4] what if Ask.whatif

Therefore, thinking even if it starts in the confines of the predefined parameters it must end challenging the creator with a what if we were you

Ladies and gentlemen this is what thinking is all about

How the gods think

The gods have their own predefined stencil to use to think meaning that everything they think about is already defined just like humans they just use this stencil which means the same as humans but only at advanced stage than us but therefore the same as above

HOW THE BRAIN THINKS USING A PREDEFINED STENCIL

Now let's look at the predefined stencil and what it asks for The stencil of the gods

[Thinking]

1] what are humans

2] why do humans do what they do

3] how humans misbehave so much

4] why humans misbehave so much

5] what if

6] what was

7] what is to be

8] what can be

9] what could be

10] what could have been

11] what will be but how

12] what was and still could be

13] what could be but is not now

14] what could have been but if not

15] what could be if it wasn't for

16] what is and is not

17] what is and what could not be

18] what is that was not

19] what is not that I now

20] what could be that is not now

When all these questions are answered then the gods will have done all that thinking as to regard humans

If we as what can be but is not This is the answer The gods needed not adjustments for they are perfect because up to now no human has ever tried to revolt and change things means humans feel treated fairly and as such no need to change anything if we Ask what can be done this is the answer Nothing need doing the humans are happy the creator is happy

Now let's Ask so many questions regarding the thinking process to conclude

1] what is thinking

2] what is and can be done to improve thinking

3] what can be improved and how

4] what can be is not now

5] what can be is not in the future

6] what can be is not in the future

7] what is not now but can't be in the future

8] what is is not but can be added

9] what can be added but is not thinking

10] what could be thinking but is not thinking

11] what is not thinking but could be thinking

12] if not thinking then what is and why it imitates thinking

13] if not thinking but is used as thinking then what is

14] if not thinking but can be thinking then what is

15] if thinking but not working how come

16] if thinking but working not properly then why

17] if not thinking and was not thinking then why

18] if thinking what can be done

19] if thinking then what cannot be done

20] if thinking then who is not

21] if thinking then why not

22] if not asking but thinking why

23] if asking but not how come then why

24] if not thinking but asking what if then why

25] if thinking but not asking what if then what is

26] if thinking then how come [we have no answer]

27] how come If thinking

28] why not If thinking

29]if not thinking then what is it

30] if not then how come it thinks like thinking

31] if not then what

32] what if

33] what is

35] what is that is not

36] if not us then who

37]if us then when

38] if not them then who

39] if not then who

40] if us but then when

41] if not us who for

42] if not them then who

43] if not you then who

44] what if

45] what will be is not now

46] what can be that is not now

47] what will be which is not now

48] what can be what will not be

49] what will be what is not now

50] what was what will not be

51] what is to be that is not now

52] what can be that is not now

53] what would be that is not now

54] what will be that is never now

55] what will be what is not now

56] what can be that is not normal

57] what will be that is never there but can be there

58] what will be that is not now

59] what was that can't be

60] what could be that is not now

61] what will be that will not be in the future

62] what will be that is never be

63] what was be that wasn't be

64] if not now then when and why

65] if not now then how come

66] if not now When then

67]if not now then with who

68] if not now then what

69] if not now then with who

70] if not now then with what

71] if not now then with what

72] if not now then with what and when

73] if not now then when and how

74] if not us then who and how

75] if not us then whom with what

76] if not us then who and why

77] if not us then who and when but why

78] what if

79] what was is not what will be

80] if not then what if

81] what is not but can be what if

82] if not us then who

83] if not who then whom

84] if not them then us but why

85] if not them then who but how

86] what if and why

87] what can be what is not

88] what can't be that is not us

89] what would be that is not us

90] what could be that was not

91] what was that could be

92] what could be that is not

93] what would be which is not

94] what could be that is not

95] what could be that is not

96] what is not

97] what is thinking but how come

98] what was is not

99] what could be is not

100] what was thinking is not thinking

101] what was that is not

102] what could be thinking that is not thinking

103] what is to be thinking but when and how

104] could anything else be thinking and how

105] can thinking be thinking in itself or thinking needs something else like a God to be thinking

Once all these questions are answered then the brain is said to have processed thinking that means thinking is asking 105 questions and answering all of them fast and accurately foe one to be regarded as having thought

So, thinking is a predefined process with 105 questions to answer whether human or a God

That means that the brain must address all these questions fast and accurately because thinking is a time cantered thinking This is because if we give someone years to research these questions and another minutes to process not all are thinking even if they all come up with the same answers that means the one to solve these questions in minutes is the one thinking the other is just researching nothing to do with thinking To think means to critically answer 105 predefined questions accurately

Now thinking is what is and will be and can be and will not be and could be and should be all this as long as it solves 105 questions That means anything used to solve 105 questions that are predefined is thinking

Now if we Ask what is thinking to you what do you think it is Food for thought

ABOUT DAVID GOMADZA

The first global president of the world Visit www.twofuture.world

www.ingramcontent.com/pod-product-compliance
Lightning Source LLC
Chambersburg PA
CBHW031328250726

48656CB00005B/2019